Rapid Weight Loss Hypnosis

Burn Fat and Lose Weight Fast, Naturally Stop Cravings, and Build Healthy Eating Habits with Powerful Self-Hypnosis, Guided Meditation, and Positive Affirmations

Rapid Weight Loss Hypnosis

PUBLISHED BY: Kaizen Mindfulness Meditations
© **Copyright 2019 - All rights reserved.**

The content contained within this book may not be reproduced, duplicated or transmitted without direct written permission from the author or the publisher.

Under no circumstances will any blame or legal responsibility be held against the publisher, or author, for any damages, reparation, or monetary loss due to the information contained within this book. Either directly or indirectly.

Legal Notice:

This book is copyright protected. This book is only for personal use. You cannot amend, distribute, sell, use, quote or paraphrase any part, or the content within this book, without the consent of the author or publisher.

Disclaimer Notice:

Please note the information contained within this document is for educational and entertainment purposes only. All effort has been executed to present accurate, up to date, and reliable, complete information. No warranties of any kind are declared or implied. Readers acknowledge that the author is not engaging in the rendering of legal, financial, medical or professional advice. The content within this book has been derived from various sources. Please consult a licensed professional before attempting any techniques outlined in this book.

By reading this document, the reader agrees that under no circumstances is the author responsible for any losses, direct or indirect, which are incurred as a result of the use of information contained within this document, including, but not limited to, — errors, omissions, or inaccuracies

Table of contents

My FREE Gifts to You 4

Introduction 6

Chapter 1 - How Hypnosis Can Help You Lose Weight 7

Chapter 2- Self Hypnosis for Weight Loss 13

Chapter 3 - Self-Hypnosis for Exercise 40

Chapter 4 - Hypnosis to Control Food Cravings 51

Chapter 5 - Positive Affirmations for Weight Loss 60

Chapter 6 - Additional Tips for Weight Loss ... 99

Conclusion 102

Thank you 104

My FREE Gifts to You

As a way of saying thanks for reading my book, I want to offer you my complete *Law of Attraction: Attract What You Desire* Boxset for FREE.

To get instant access just go to:

https://theartofmastery.com/loa

This boxset includes:

1. *Law of Attraction: Attract What You Desire* eBook
2. *Law of Attraction: Attract What You Desire* audiobook

3. LOA workbook with guided exercises
4. LOA checklist
5. Mind maps
6. 20 of the best LOA quotes posters
7. 20 of the best LOA affirmation posters

Get instant access at:
https://theartofmastery.com/loa

Introduction

First, I want to congratulate you for choosing this book because that means you're getting serious to improving the quality of your life.

It takes a lot of faith, commitment, and courage to take the leap, so I highly commend you.

I strongly believe that the greatest investment you can make is not in any business, or real estate, or in the stock market - but in yourself. If you are not at your optimum level, it can be quite difficult to do well in any area of your life.

Choosing this book is your first step in losing weight, which is a very big investment in yourself.

This audiobook will guide you through hypnosis and positive affirmations that are designed to help you rewire your brain so you can prepare your body towards weight loss.

Once again, thanks for purchasing this book, I hope you find it to be helpful!

Chapter 1 - How Hypnosis Can Help You Lose Weight

Hypnosis is mainly used in hypnotherapy, which is a form of alternative medicine for the treatment of certain health problems such as smoking, alcoholism, stress, and even obesity.

Hypnosis can be self-induced or administered by a hypnotherapist who is trained to tap the subconscious mind in order to change the mindset of the patient.

When you are under hypnosis, your body and mind enter an enhanced state of awareness that makes you more open to powerful suggestions.

So through hypnotherapy, your mind can accept new insights that can help in rewiring your brain towards significant changes such as setting your mind towards weight loss.

The goal of hypnosis is to harmonize both the conscious and subconscious areas of your brain that will better empower it for control over your behavior and emotions.

This empowerment is accomplished through verbal repetition and mental imagery, which opens the mind.

Hypnosis Prepare Your Body for Weight Loss

Losing weight is not an easy task. It takes a lot of physical and mental fortitude to achieve such a feat.

Therefore, it is crucial for you to prepare your mind so you can see faster results. Through regular self-hypnosis, you are gradually declogging your mind to clear away negative thoughts and self-defeating beliefs about weight loss.

And while hypnosis can prepare your mind to achieve weight loss, positive affirmations can help you reinforce your will and resolve to stay on course.

That is why, in this audiobook, you will have a chance to listen to both hypnosis and positive affirmations to help you achieve your goal.

The Science behind Using Hypnosis for Weight Loss

The fundamental idea behind hypnotherapy is that our brains can be rewired to modify habits like stress-eating.

In a study published in the International Journal of Obesity (IJO) in 1998, scientists studied the use of hypnosis for weight loss in subjects who were suffering from sleep apnea.

Researchers examined two forms of hypnosis as opposed to regular diet advised for weight loss and sleep apnea. After three months, the subjects were able to lose at least 2% of their body weight. But after 18 months, the subjects who were also treated with hypnosis lost another 8% of their body weight.

The same journal also published another study in 2005 wherein scientists evaluated the results of hypnosis used through Cognitive Behavioral

Therapy (CBT). The subjects who were under CBT lost a higher percentage of body weight compared to subjects who were under placebo.

Are You Willing to Try Hypnotherapy?

Although the area of using hypnosis for losing weight should be scrutinized through more research, more and more people can already attest to its advantages.

If you are doubtful of this alternative then it may not be the right solution for you. Remember, hypnotherapy requires your willingness. It may not work for you if you develop resistance within your mind.

So please, if you are really serious about losing weight and you want to try hypnosis to rewire your brain, then this is the perfect time to have an open mind.

Most people who are trying to lose weight usually want to get fast results. However, it is not always healthy to lose weight at a quick rate.

Unfortunately, you will get back the extra pounds lost as soon as you stopped following these diet fads. Losing weight must be a steady and slow process, and this is where hypnotherapy can significantly help.

Hypnosis may benefit you if you are among those people who often get attracted to diet fads because they promise quick results.

Through hypnosis, you can rewire your brain and get into a healthier lifestyle. This is a great alternative to invasive surgeries such as liposuction or gastric bypass surgery that present many significant risks.

The Benefits of Hypnotherapy for Losing Weight

Basically, hypnosis that is geared towards weight loss can help you develop a more positive image about yourself. The session usually starts with accepting your situation and doing something about it not because of peer pressure but because of health reasons.

Hypnosis will reframe your mind and will help you better understand your "why" or the reason behind your goal for weight loss. This alternative session will help you manage your weight because it directly taps your motives and self-interest.

Another benefit of hypnotherapy for weight loss is it can help you relieve stress. The meditative component of hypnosis can help you achieve a calmer and more relaxed mind. Relieving stress is important in weight loss as there are studies showing the connection between stress and an increase in appetite.

Hypnotherapy will also rewire your conscious and subconscious mind so you can feel good about exercise and healthy diets. These two components go hand in hand in weight loss, and through hypnosis, you will see them as allies and not as a burden.

Chapter 2- Self Hypnosis for Weight Loss

We will formally start a general self-hypnosis to help rewire your brain and prepare your body for rapid weight loss.

Just remember that self-hypnosis requires you to be open and willing. It may not work for you if your mind is already opposed to it.

Before the actual hypnosis, you should first find a comfortable and quiet room to start the session.

Find a room that is free from noise and where no one can disturb you. Wear comfortable clothes and make sure that the room is neither too hot nor too cold.

Now, breathe deeply. Begin with five deep breaths, inhaling through your nose and exhaling through your mouth.

As you exhale, imagine that all your stress are coming out of your body.

Allow this feeling to move down from your head to your shoulders...to your chest...to your arms...to your stomach...to your legs...and finally...to your feet.

You can start relaxing now and just take this time to wind down. Let all that tension you feel be gone.

Even if I am guiding you now, this is not something that I can do to you or for you but instead, hypnosis is achieving a state of deep relaxation, by yourself.

In this state of relaxation, the mind suspends all its critical faculties so that my suggestions will be beneficial and true for you.

Your deeper subconscious mind will accept and receive all the things I will say to you.

After all, trance is an everyday natural calming experience. And in this hypnosis, I am just going to help you learn how to achieve that experience effortlessly.

Start by asking yourself if you have experienced a calm relaxed state prior to this moment.

Try to recall relaxing or calming experiences that you have felt in the past. Perhaps some hobbies you find relaxing or a holiday you can never forget.

Focus on bringing those experiences to your mind and remember the positive feelings you have felt before.

Now, you have to go into a deeper trance while sitting down where you are or lying down in bed with your head comfortably down in a soft pillow.

Slowly, you can go deeper into a state of hypnotic calm.

Try to ask yourself, do you want to have your eyes open?

I'll have them closed.

Are you willing to experience this deeper sense of calming relaxation?

You can relax even deeper knowing that your inner and outer world are in harmony and helping you achieve deeper relaxation.

As you go deeper, you feel yourself sinking into that chair or perhaps as you lie there, your entire body lets all that tension flow out.

I wonder if you've already realized how easy it is to let your mind drift away into this calming hypnotic state?

You can watch yourself doing this now almost as if you are stepping outside of your physical body.

Just a little way outside of your own body...watching your own physical form...relaxing...just in that specific way however you choose...just drifting along into a trance.

There is no right or wrong way...just relax and dream...

Close your eyes so you can relax even more. You can let your inner mind close...or perhaps open it up. It's your choice. You are still in control.

I am just your guiding voice.

I don't know exactly where your subconscious mind is bringing you now.

Although you hear my voice inside, you should know that I am part of your outer world.

You are still in control.

But with your permission, my voice can tap your subconscious mind so it will be open to suggestions that will bring you positive results.

As my voice goes deeper into your subconscious mind, you will start to see images that may bring you mixed feelings or emotions - happiness, joy, guilt, shame, pride, anger, or even love.

Try to filter the emotions and choose the positive ones. You need these emotions so you can achieve a more relaxed state.

As you choose to feel only positive emotions, you will feel lighter. You will feel that you are just floating.

This is a sign that your subconscious mind is opening up and letting go. This is a sign that you are unleashing your worries.

This will help you be mindful of what you feel. You are just concerned with the present moment and you can just allow all the sounds that you hear and the thoughts you think to pass by without paying them any attention.

At this moment, your subconscious mind is allowing itself to focus more and more deeply on its own inner unconscious reality.

I'm not sure if you have really and genuinely experienced this level of deep relaxation.

Perhaps, you find this odd because you may feel you are drifting and just floating into oblivion.

You may feel that you are not in control, but you don't feel a bit worried.

In fact, you feel that you are happy now that you feel deeply relaxed because you've made a conscious decision...to take this time...to go inside...and explore your own inner world.

And I do know that this can be a truly rewarding experience... an experience where you can learn something of considerable value...things that are really positive...which might help you to overcome any particular difficulties that you are currently undergoing right now.

This session is helping you see through the veil of illusion that will help you to really live and genuinely live as you choose.

As you go deeper into a trance, visualize that you are standing at the top of a grand staircase.

What is it made of?

Is it made of wood? stone? or steel?

What's the color of the staircase you see?

Can you smell the texture of the staircase? Can you feel the texture of the banister underneath your right hand?

As you stand at the top of this beautiful staircase, you look down and see that it has ten descending steps.

You can see the color of the carpet covering the stairs and you find yourself standing barefoot on the soft carpet.

As you go down the stairs in just a moment from now, I'm going to count them down for you...step by step.

And perhaps you'd like to follow along...

Count along with me in your own mind, and as you say the number for each step, you can give yourself the suggestion to go deeper into your relaxation.

Reach out your hand and place it onto that smooth banister guiding you down.

You take that first step and just let yourself relax deeper down now...

The more you relax, the better you feel...

You become even more sleepy and drowsy...

You now feel that shift down in your own internal state...

It feels as if you are shifting down gears in your car to drift down...

We are now in the 8th step, and we go deeper and deeper down...

And now onto the seventh step towards deeper relaxation...

You will notice that the color of that carpet is becoming even deeper...

Even deeper as you step down onto the sixth step...

Stepping down five...halfway there to your total relaxation...

And with every deep breath that you take now...and then exhale...you find yourself relaxing...more and more...

It just feels so wonderfully good to let your bare feet sink into that thick and rich carpet...

As you go down the stairs even further into this wonderful relaxation...

Deeply...

Drowsy...

Sleepy...

Sleepy state of trance...

You can look forward to going into an even deeper state perhaps the deepest state of relaxation.

You can even remember now...

And three...

Doubling your relaxation...

Now in the next number I say, you can step down and find yourself in the deepest level of relaxation that you've experienced for quite some time.

And two... you can feel more relaxed now...

And now one..relaxing...relaxing down...so so far down...

And as you continue to drift and dream along just floating lightly to wherever it is that your mind is taking you now...

Perhaps you can imagine yourself walking along a beautiful white sandy beach...

As you look around, you know that it is in the middle of spring...

And it is just perfect and nice...and not too warm not too cool...just a perfect day on this beautiful beach.

The sky is brilliant blue and the sun is a golden blazing yellow touching down your skin...

And again you find yourself standing barefoot on this glistening white sand feeling that cold wet firm and hard-packed sand beneath your toes...

And you can taste the smell of the salt in the air...

And you can feel the residue of salt depositing on your lips from the cool ocean spray...

All the time feeling wonderfully good...

You can taste the salt of the sea on your lips and you can hear the beating of those gentle waves...

And as each wave rolls in, you find yourself sinking deeper and deeper into relaxation just farther and farther down...

You feel really wonderfully good...

As each wave rolls out into the blue sea, it carries with it all of the remaining tension in your body...

Each wave carries away all the things that your body doesn't really need anymore.

And as you watch all of that tension just drifting away towards the horizon, you can see the giant sun beginning to set down...

The warm sun casts its beautiful orange rays across the entire beach.

With every gentle wave, you find yourself sinking more and more into comfort and serenity.

Every gentle wave carries with it every remaining tension that you wish to discard from your life...

And while you are aware that this state of relaxation will be for a short while, you know that you have plenty of time to become completely relaxed...

Now as you walk on this sunset beach and you already kissed goodbye to your worries, you are now more capable of relaxing as you breathe more easily and more gently...

You can feel the calmness entering your body and all of the tension leaving once more.

It's almost as if you can watch your own mind becoming calmer just like the surface of a silent ocean...

Your mind reflects all of the beautiful sunset just without any ripples at all...now...just a flat smooth ocean.

Calm and relaxed...and as you continue to walk along this orange sunset beach...you can see up ahead that there is a wooden bench.

Just sit on this bench as you feel the gentle waves on your feet.

The bench is made of wood but it is surprisingly comfortable and made just the way you like it.

And as you sink down into this wonderful cushioning, you find yourself drifting away even more into this.

You feel safe, and you are at peace.

You feel safe, and you are comfortable.

You feel safe and you are happy.

You feel safe and you feel relaxed.

Because you are letting your mind now just spontaneously take you to a new place, anything is possible for you.

You may find yourself in a place that you go regularly or you may find yourself in a place that you have visited once in the past but quite memorable.

You may also visit a place that is completely imaginary - perhaps a place that you really want to visit but haven't gone there in your waking world.

You should know that any place is fine. Whatever comes into your mind now...and if you find that your mind goes from one place to another, you know that those are just gentle tricks of your mind.

You are just being played by the conscious part of your own being.

One part of your thinking mind says that this is impossible, illogical, and pure fantasy. This part of your rational mind is judgmental and will lead you to an external rather than an internal experience.

What was the first place that you have seen?

Because this place appeared in your mind spontaneously, this is the place that you really choose to stay with.

Because this place was conjured by your deeper subconscious mind, you feel safe.

As you visualize this place, you even focus on these words...peace, safety, happiness, lightness, and joy.

And you can take the time now to appreciate this scene with all of your senses because you notice all of those unique things about this very safe place...and all around you as a protective magical bubble.

As you can imagine it vividly now, this protective bubble is just as large or as medium or as small as you choose to make it

Surprisingly, you can still hear the sounds of your safe place within this protective bubble.

You may even choose to reach out and touch the surface of that bubble feeling its protective yet comfortable layer.

What's the color of the protective bubble you see around yourself now? Is it blue or green or purple or yellow? Or some other beautiful colors of the rainbow?

As you explore all the finer details of this magical place, you know that whether it be outside the protective bubble or inside, you are in control over who or what can enter the bubble.

This includes everything like air or water or emotions or even people you care about or really want to stay away from.

As you choose which things you want to enter your bubble, you realize that you have so much power and control over this place.

You have so much personal power.

You have so much ownership of your own true being.

As you drift along, you realize that your favorite place and the magical protective bubble will become increasingly associated with the important, deeper parts of your unconscious mind.

You become more aware of important concepts of peace, safety, acceptance, comfort, joy, and happiness.

You know that as time goes by, all of these associations will only strengthen your subconscious mind.

You can visit your favorite place mentally just as soon as you choose.

You can also completely dissociate yourself from whatever is happening to you in your waking consciousness.

Your mind can control your body.

You will feel more relaxed during times of stress, and you will feel lighter than your actual weight.

This will help you avoid stress, so you are happier and you feel more positive that you can achieve your weight loss goal.

As you intensify your practice for hypnotherapy, you can easily conjure your protective bubble even in your waking state.

Your mind will become stronger and more powerful to the extent that you can automatically feel the comfort, relaxation, quietness, and peace that you are experiencing now.

You can practice this image just by thinking of your protective bubble several times each day in your usual waking state.

You will remember that each time you visit your favorite place, the protective bubble becomes stronger.

And so your mind becomes stronger. It will become easier for you to achieve all of the benefits of this positive image.

As you become more familiar with this positive image that you are witnessing now, your subconscious mind will start the gradual process of imprinting this into your mind.

This will help you create a more positive change in your life as you become more active in your waking life.

Whenever you are presented with choices - to either be healthy or be lazy - your subconscious mind will tap this positive image.

As your subconscious mind remembers the positive image you are witnessing now, your mind will be more in control of your eating habits.

Your mind will boost your will power, so you can say no to unhealthy habits. Your subconscious mind will be alerted if you are eating more than your body needs and if your body needs to be active.

And you know that the mind controls your own eating, almost as if you are in your own control room.

As you visit your inner world to strengthen your mental fortitude, you can easily access this control room.

Eventually, you become more familiar with the dials, controls, and levers that you can move up and down.

You have so much control and power over your own eating.

You know that whatever you put in your mouth, exactly when and how much you choose to eat is now controlled by you in this control room.

This control room is now part of your deeper and genuine self...

It is not your stomach or your appetite that really controls what you eat.

It is really your own mind and you can ask the deeper part of your mind any time.

Beginning today, it is time to develop new habits for yourself and to set yourself new positive goals.

Through this hypnosis, you are building the mental foundation that is crucial to help you achieve your weight loss goal.

Through your subconscious mind, you can easily see a more positive you.

You now eat so much less...

You are aware that the less you eat, the happier you feel.

The less you eat, the more that you can smile and be successful in your career.

And now the less you eat, the more relaxed you are.

And now the less you eat, the better you look and the better you feel.

And now the less you eat, the more patient you are. You are more cheerful with yourself and with the people around you.

And now the less you eat the more you have the motivation to succeed.

And now the less you eat, the more energy you can have.

Kaizen Mindfulness Meditations

And now you find satisfaction in eating less, you can pride yourself in knowing that each time that you do, you are rewarding your slimmer, healthier natural self.

Your healthy self wants to be the more energetic and active slimmer you.

And you know now that your slimmer self already exists deep within you.

And whenever you choose this new image of yourself, you experience new feelings of health and calmness and positive well-being.

You are convinced that it feels good to feel good about yourself.

It is simply amazing that you are now in control of your eating habits.

Remember, you are eating because you need to live.

You are not living so you can eat.

Now, it is easier to eat healthily and sensibly because you are gaining new strength.

Your newfound strength will help you eat healthier food and be more sensible in your choices.

And you eat sensibly and find yourself still satisfied.

As you exercise this new strength, you will find that it grows and grows...

You will discover that you are now more capable to resist any unhealthy temptation.

This growing resolve becomes a more natural part of your true identity.

This mental resolve is similar to your muscles. The more you use them, the more they become stronger and stronger.

As you eat sensibly each day, it becomes easier and easier to continue on in a practical, healthy, and positive way.

Through this hypnosis, you can program your mind to mentally ask your own body first if a type of food you are about to eat is good for you.

Your subconscious mind will start learning how to listen to your body as it checks first if the food you want to eat is really healthy.

Or exactly how much or how little food your body actually and truly needs from time to time.

Be aware that proper eating is always eating slowly and carefully.

You need to savor the flavor of your food and concentrate on chewing them.

Always be conscious when chewing your food.

Eating and drinking properly means taking in just enough for your own body now.

As you find yourself exercising better and eating properly, your body becomes automatically regulated to reach the ideal size and weight.

Your brain is starting to rewire itself to direct your body to be just as slim as you wish to be.

By using your deeper creative imagination, you can now visualize yourself just as you choose to be.

You can create this positive mental image of yourself just precisely the way you really wish to be.

You can achieve the way you want to look exactly the way you wish to feel.

You can even mentally dress in the clothes you want to wear.

You can bring that image of yourself wearing your ideal clothes.

You can feel wonderfully good knowing that you choose to be this way.

This session will prepare your body to be more physically active.

You can start with five minutes, then increase your physical activity to 10 minutes, then 30 minutes, until you can improve your level of activity into an hour.

You are now rewiring your brain to feel good when you are moving.

Your mind feels wonderful when you are active.

Your body feels wonderful when you are healthy and fit.

And you see yourself using your new energy now in a positive, constructive way.

And you can feel this energy spreading and growing throughout your body...

You feel warm and comfort just like those rays of the sun touching down into your skin and warming you from head to toe with this new positive and vibrant energy.

Visualize your own bathroom scales or any set of weighing scale you use.

Mentally place on the scale the exact number that you wish your body will truly weigh.

Just take the time now to visualize that from happening or try to see that you have already achieved that weight.

Because you feel wonderfully good seeing that you already achieved it....that you already reached your ideal weight.

Because you have already increased your physical activity and you already look exactly the way you wish you could look, and that has a profound impact on your subconscious mind now.

You are already feeling so positive, and you are already so incredibly proud of your own results because you have become exactly the way you wish to truly look and feel.

And as you rewire your mind to think that your body is becoming healthy, your body is actually starting the process of becoming healthy.

Your subconscious mind knows that health is an important part of the new you.

Your subconscious mind chooses to breathe clean air and you choose to eat healthy food.

And later when you open your eyes once again, your mind will remember that you no longer have to overeat and you no longer have to be hungry.

Because when you think of something to eat and it is not yet time to eat, your mind will immediately remind you of something better to do.

Your mind is stronger now to resist unhealthy eating habits and your body is a lot stronger to pursue activities that can help you feel energized and satisfied.

And it can be whatever you truly wish to do something that really satisfies you.

And you can enjoy whatever it is that you do even if it is by yourself.

Because you find yourself fun when you are fit and you find yourself acceptable, you'll love and accept yourself.

And you find yourself fun to be with now.

As you tune in to your true authentic self, you know that you can understand yourself at a deeper level and you are learning to love and accept yourself.

You are learning to love and accept yourself on a deeper level now.

And you know that your loving self will accept what you truly are and what you really wish to become.

Your authentic true self deserves to feel completely healthy and you treat yourself exactly as you choose to treat someone whom you love and respect.

And someone whom you accept completely because your deeper self deserves all of your healthy loving energy.

And you find that the more that you learn to love and accept yourself, the easier it becomes to develop your own positive changes in your life.

And just as you are developing a new healthy energized attitude for yourself, you know that you are on the right path.

Because just as you find yourself thinking yourself happier, you find yourself feeling happier.

And perhaps even other people are telling you how good you look.

Perhaps even other people are telling you how inspiring you are to them to encourage them to feel positive and healthy in every way.

Because you know that you're taking the time now to really enjoy preparing your own healthy food with a loving and positive self-accepting attitude...

You feel better as you take the time to just accept and integrate all of these ideas on a deeper level.

If you are listening to this in the evening and you choose to drift off to a deeper sleep, you can just drift off now.

Just feel wonderfully good allowing your body to drift down and completely let go into that true deeper sound and restful sleep.

But if you are listening to this during the day or evening when you need to get up once again and continue on with your activities then in a moment I'm going to count upwards from one to five.

And when I reach five, you can open your eyes completely and come back to full conscious waking reality.

And so one...allow yourself to gently come back towards conscious waking reality.

And two...come back gradually and slowly to complete awareness

And three…take a nice deep relaxing calm breath.

And four…let your eyes open as if they had been both in crystal clear fresh spring water.

And five…open your eyes completely and adjust yourself again to your waking surrounding feeling wonderfully good and energized.

You now feel refreshed, relaxed, and ready to continue your activities, but your mind is now stronger than before.

Thank you for listening once again and talk to you soon.

Chapter 3 - Self-Hypnosis for Exercise

The hypnosis that you have heard in the previous chapter is generally used to rewire your brain as a way to prepare yourself for rapid weight loss.

Remember, effective weight loss is heavily dependent on two pillars: regular exercise and a healthy diet.

In this chapter, you will access your mind towards better motivation to sustain the needed exercise for weight loss.

Hypnosis works by means of making both mind and body relaxed towards a comfortable and safe level. This lets direct communication with the subconscious mind.

The subconscious mind regulates and controls body temperature and stores emotions and memories.

Hypnotherapists generally tap the subconscious mind to help you access your emotions and memories.

The subconscious mind is also the part of the mind that asks no questions, has no perceptions, opinions or views, and has no ability to distinguish between what's right or wrong, true or false.

Hypnosis has the ability to restructure and redefine deeply rooted emotions within the subconscious mind.

This change can be manifested in your waking reality.

In a few moments, the hypnosis will begin but before that, I would just like to remind you that this recording contains powerful hypnotic suggestions.

This session may cause deep relaxation and sometimes sleep.

So please be sure that wherever you are listening to this audiobook, you should be in a safe and comfortable environment where you are able to fully relax and let go.

Now start by finding a nice comfortable chair. Take a seat and relax.

You will simply ignore the everyday noises such as passing vehicles or telephones ringing. But if you hear any alarm bells or sounds of danger, you will instantly awaken.

Concentrate on your breathing...take it slowly. You will notice that you are more relaxed with every breath you take.

Your mind will naturally drift away with numerous thoughts, but let them pass and try to concentrate on my voice.

And relax...just allow any thoughts to drift away...

Relax...

Let your whole body sink into the comfortable relaxing chair...

Let the chair carry your full body weight...

Allow your mind to unwind and be fully relaxed...

Then, slowly let go of everything that is weighing you down...

Every bit of stress, worry, and strain...

This is now the best time to let go...

Let's start with your feet.

Just relax and allow the muscles in your feet to completely relax. Notice how happy they feel and how relaxed they are now...

Now moving to your legs...let them fully relax.

Notice how your legs become weak and tired...

Now moving up to your back and arms, you will notice how relaxed the muscles in your back feel...

Also, notice how any stress or worries simply drift away...

Just allow any stress or worries to drift away...

Moving up to your shoulders...just let go of any tension that may have built up in your shoulders...

Allow your muscles to loosen and then breathe deeply...

You will realize that by doing this, you are allowing yourself to fully relax and be more peaceful...just relax...

Lastly, moving up to your head...focus all your attention on the muscles in your head...in your face, cheeks, and jaw.

Allow your muscles to relax and drop...

Now, visualize yourself standing at the top of a staircase.

What is the staircase made of? Wood? Stone? Steel?

Can you smell the staircase? Can you feel its texture?

As you look down, you will see that this staircase has 10 steps and you are standing at the top...on the 10th step.

In a few moments, I'm going to ask you to walk down these steps...

With each step you walk down, you will feel even more relaxed...

So, moving down to step 9, feeling more and more relaxed...moving down to step 8...and step 7...notice how with every step you take, you become even more relaxed...

And now to step 6...step 5...step 4... drifting deeper and deeper...step 3...and down to step 2....and step 1.

Now that you have descended the staircase, you will see a doorway that leads up to a beautiful garden.

I'd like you to walk through this doorway and into the garden.

Notice how beautiful and peaceful it feels...

Notice the flowers and the trees and all the different shapes you see...just immerse yourself in the beautiful surroundings.

Look down at the grass and see how healthy and fresh they are...

Sit on the grass and become aware of how soft and comfortable you are...

Feel the warm air against your skin from the top of your head...

Feel the warm air and the soft ground...feel the power of relaxation...

Enjoy this feeling of relaxation for a few minutes and relax...

Now, your mind has become centered and so receptive to what I say...

Everything I say will sink deeply into your subconscious mind...

All the information that you need to succeed in your goal will be stored deeply within your mind...

With every hour of every day, that goes by, you will become more motivated and energized...

When you exercise, you feel good...you are full of energy

When you exercise, you feel a rush of endorphins...

When you exercise, you feel strong...

When you exercise, you feel that you are filled with energy...

Exercise makes you look and feel great...you are full of positive energy...you are full of energy...

Exercise makes your body look more attractive...

Suddenly, you have the urge to exercise....

When you exercise, you are capable of pushing yourself to reach your personal and work goals...

You now enjoy exercising as often as possible...you are full of energy...

When you exercise, you are full of endorphins...

Being healthy makes you feel good about yourself...

You are a strong person that is capable of exercising on a regular basis...

You are capable of achieving anything you want as long as you set your mind to it...

You have full belief in yourself and in your abilities...

Exercise is good for you and makes you a strong person...

Your levels of energy and motivation will become more defined as time goes by...

With every hour of every day, you will become more motivated and energized...

When you exercise, you feel good...you are full of energy.

When you exercise, you feel a rush of endorphins...you feel strong and full of energy...

Exercise makes you look great...

Exercise makes your body look more attractive...

You feel happy after exercising...

Being fit and healthy makes you feel amazing...

You are able to push yourself to reach your goals...

You enjoy exercising as often as possible...

You are full of energy.

Exercising makes you healthy...

You have the motivation to reach your full potential...

You feel strong...you are full of energy...

When you exercise, you are full of endorphins...

Being healthy makes you feel good about yourself...you are a strong person who is capable of exercising on a regular basis...

You can achieve anything you set your mind to...you are always motivated and full of energy.

Exercise is good for you and makes you strong...

With every hour of every day...you will become more motivated and energized...

When you exercise, you feel good...you are full of energy...

When you exercise, you feel a rush of endorphins...

So strong and full of energy...Exercise makes you look and feel great...

You are full of positive energy...full of youthful energy...

Exercise makes your body more attractive...

You feel happy after exercising...

Being fit and healthy makes you feel amazing...

You are able to push yourself to reach your goals...

You enjoy exercising as often as possible...

Exercising makes you healthy...

You have the motivation to reach your full potential...

You feel strong and full of energy...

When you exercise, you are full of energy...

Being healthy makes you feel good about yourself...

You are a very strong person who is capable of exercising on a regular basis...

You can change anything you set your mind to...

You are always motivated and full of energy...

You have full belief in yourself...

Exercise is good for you and makes you a strong person...

Your levels of energy and motivation will become more defined as time goes by...

You have the motivation to reach your full potential...

When you exercise, you are full of endorphins...

You are a strong person who is capable of exercising on a regular basis...

You can achieve anything you set your mind to...

You are motivated in all situations...

And as the days and weeks go by, you feel motivated...

You will grow more powerful and more defined...

In a few moments, I'm going to awaken you. I'm going to count to 10.

And on the number five, you will begin to wake up.

In number eight, you will open your eyes.

And when we reach 10, you will be wide awake and you will feel only positive thoughts...

So one... two... three... four... five...

starting to wake up now...

six... seven... eight... open your eyes...

nine... ten... wide awake...

And welcome back...

I hope you enjoyed this session.

You should listen to this session as often as possible to ensure maximum results...

I wish you success in your goal to achieve weight loss through regular exercise...

Thank you for listening...

Chapter 4 - Hypnosis to Control Food Cravings

Hello and welcome to our hypnosis session to control food cravings.

You are listening to this session to control food cravings and stop from binge eating...

Before we begin, please take note that this recording contains powerful hypnotic suggestions that may cause deep relaxation and sometimes, sleep...

So please be sure that wherever you are listening to this recording, you are in a safe and comfortable environment where you are able to fully relax and let go...

Now start by finding a nice comfortable chair. Take a seat and relax.

And take a deep breath.

You will simply ignore any day to day noises such as passing vehicles or ringing telephones...

But you will instantly awaken if you hear any alarm bells or any sound of danger...

Now, try to focus on your breathing...

Breathe slowly…

You will feel that with each moment passing by, you will feel more relaxed…

Just allow any thoughts that come into your mind to drift away…

Just focus on my voice and relax…

Allow any thoughts to drift away and relax…

Allow yourself to rest into the comfortable and calming chair or bed…

Let the chair carry the weight of your body…

As you relax, let your mind fully relax and unwind…

Let go of everything that causes you anxiety or stress…

Just relax…

Let's start with your feet.

Just relax and allow the muscles to completely relax.

Notice how happy they feel and how relaxed they are now…

Now moving to your legs…let them fully relax.

Pay attention to how weak and tired they feel…

Now moving up to your back and arms...

Notice how relaxed the muscles in your back feel...

Notice how any stress or worries simply drift away...

Just allow any stress or worries to drift away...

Moving up to your shoulders...just let go of any tension that may have built up in your shoulders...

Allow your muscles to loosen and then breathe deeply...

You will realize that by doing this, you are allowing yourself to fully relax and be more peaceful...

Just relax...

Lastly, moving up to your head...focus all your attention on the muscles in your head...in your face, cheeks, and jaw.

Allow your muscles to relax and drop...

Now, visualize yourself standing at the top of a staircase.

This staircase has ten steps and you are standing at the top...on the 10th step.

In a few moments, I'm going to ask you to walk down these steps...with each step you walk down, you will feel even more relaxed...

So, moving down to step 9, feeling more and more relaxed...

Moving down to step 8...and step 7...

Notice how with every step you take you become even more relaxed...

Now to step 6...step 5...step 4... drifting deeper and deeper...

Step 3...and down to step 2...and step 1...

Now that you have descended the staircase, you will see a doorway that leads up to a beautiful garden.

I'd like you to walk through this doorway and into the garden.

Notice how beautiful and peaceful it feels.

Notice the flowers and the trees and all the different shapes you see...

Just immerse yourself in the beautiful surroundings...

Look down at the grass and see how healthy and fresh they are...

Kaizen Mindfulness Meditations

Sit on the grass and become aware of how soft and comfortable you are...

Feel the warm air against your skin from the top of your head...

Feel the warm air and the soft ground...

Feel the power of relaxation...

Enjoy this feeling of relaxation for a few minutes and relax...

Now, your mind has become centered and so receptive to what I say...

Everything I say will sink deeply into your subconscious mind...

All the information that you need to succeed in your goal will be stored deeply within your mind...

You are able to control the amount of food that you eat...

You are a powerful person...

You are able to stop yourself from binge eating...

You are a positive person...

You are able to stop eating when you feel full...

The only time you need to eat is when you are hungry...

Overeating is about feelings...it makes you feel happy...

But you are so strong that you are able to control your food cravings.

You do not need to eat junk food...

You are able to express your emotions easily...

You have excellent willpower and motivation...

You are able to control the amount of food that you eat...

You are able to stop yourself from binge eating...

You are a positive person...

You are able to stop eating when you feel full...

You are capable of achieving anything as long as you set your mind to it...

The only time you need to eat is when you are hungry...

Overeating is about feelings...it makes you feel happy...

But you are so strong that you are able to control your food cravings...

You are able to eat in moderation...

You enjoy taking care of your body...

You do not need to eat junk food...

You are able to express your emotions easily...

You are able to stop yourself from overeating...

You are able to control the amount of food that you eat...

You are able to stop yourself from binge eating..

You are a positive person...

You are able to stop eating when you feel full...

You are able to do anything you set your mind to...

Nutrition is the only goal why you are eating...

Overeating is about feelings...it makes you feel happy...

But you are so strong that you are able to control your food cravings...

You are able to eat in moderation. ..

You are able to express your emotions easily. ..

You are able to control the amount of food that you eat...

You are a powerful person. You are able to stop eating when you feel full...

Overeating is about feelings...it makes you feel happy...

But you are so strong that you are able to control your food cravings.

You are able to express your emotions easily...

Stop yourself from overeating...

You are able to control the amount of food you eat.

You are a powerful person...

You are able to stop yourself from binge eating...

You are a positive person...

Nutrition is your only goal why you need to eat...

Overeating is bad for your body...

You are able to eat in moderation...

You are able to express your emotions easily...

You have excellent motivation...

You are able to control the amount of food that you eat...

You are a positive person. You are able to stop eating when you feel full...

Nutrition is your only purpose why you need to eat...

You are able to control food cravings...

You are able to eat in moderation...

In a few moments, I'm going to awaken you. I'm going to count to 10.

And on the number five you will begin to wake up.

In number eight, you will open your eyes.

And when we reach 10, you will be wide awake and you will feel positive thoughts...

So one... two... three... four... five...

starting to wake up now...

six... seven... eight... open your eyes...

nine... ten... wide awake..

And welcome back...

I hope you enjoyed this session.

You should listen to this session as often as possible to ensure maximum results...

I wish you success in your goal to achieve weight loss through proper diet and nutrition...

Thank you for listening...

Chapter 5 - Positive Affirmations for Weight Loss

Aside from hypnosis, positive affirmations also work in rewiring your brain towards weight loss.

Affirmations refer to positive statements that can help you to overcome negative thoughts. When you regularly repeat them, you tend to believe them, and you start to make positive changes.

Similar to the way we regularly exercise to improve our physical health, positive mental repetitions can reprogram our thinking patterns so that we gradually start to think and act differently.

What's the Difference between Hypnosis and Positive Affirmations?

Basically, affirmations are ideas that you repeat to yourself. They became popular in the early 1920s through the advocacy of Emil Coue who was one of the pioneers of hypnotherapy.

However, positive affirmations were called autosuggestions, in which people would be placed under a trance (usually for hours) and then the affirmations would start.

The autosuggestions were used within the frame of hypnotism and it really dwells inside the realm of hypnotism.

But as time goes by, some hypnotherapy groups and individuals took away the hypnotic element and focused on the positive statements. These statements are later on called affirmations.

Positive affirmations are now used to regularly motivate people who want to change their habits or achieve certain goals such as weight loss.

Positive affirmations are usually performed with full awareness and in verbal repetition.

On the other hand, hypnosis is performed in trance state induced through a hypnotic music. In positive affirmations, you are encouraged to follow along, while in hypnosis sessions, you don't need to say anything and you just need to listen to the voice of the speaker.

If this is your first time listening to positive affirmations, you might be surprised that the terms are repeated at least three times. Remember, repetition is key in positive affirmations.

In fact, positive affirmations work because they are entering your mind repeatedly and each repeated line reinforces the positive suggestions that your mind receives.

In this chapter and the succeeding ones, you will be able to listen to positive affirmations to prepare your mind for weight loss and specifically motivate yourself for exercise and stop food cravings.

General Positive Affirmations for Weight Loss

I am fit and healthy...

I am fit and healthy...

I am fit and healthy...

My body finds it easy to lose excess fat...

My body finds it easy to lose excess fat...

My body finds it easy to lose excess fat...

My mind is already set to healthy weight loss...

My mind is already set to healthy weight loss...

My mind is already set to healthy weight loss...

My metabolism turns up when I need it to...

My metabolism turns up when I need it to...

My metabolism turns up when I need it to...

I love myself and my body...

I love myself and my body...

I love myself and my body...

I enjoy taking care of the health of my body...

I enjoy taking care of the health of my body...

I enjoy taking care of the health of my body...

My health and well-being are a high priority for me...

My health and well-being are a high priority for me...

My health and well-being are a high priority for me...

I put myself first when it comes to my health...

I put myself first when it comes to my health...

I put myself first when it comes to my health...

I enjoy being thin and healthy...

I enjoy being thin and healthy...

I enjoy being thin and healthy...

I declare freedom from negative thoughts that keep me from being healthy...

I declare freedom from negative thoughts that keep me from being healthy...

I declare freedom from negative thoughts that keep me from being healthy...

I am at my ideal weight...

I am at my ideal weight...

My life is dedicated to healthy living...

My life is dedicated to healthy living...

My life is dedicated to healthy living...

My incredible mind returns me to my naturally thin state...

My incredible mind returns me to my naturally thin state...

My incredible mind returns me to my naturally thin state...

Every cell of my body is healthy....

Every cell of my body is healthy....

Every cell of my body is healthy....

Every cell of my body wants me to be thin and healthy...

Every cell of my body wants me to be thin and healthy...

Every cell of my body wants me to be thin and healthy...

It's automatic for me to be naturally thin...

It's automatic for me to be naturally thin...

It's automatic for me to be naturally thin...

I unconsciously make the right food choices...

I unconsciously make the right food choices...

I unconsciously make the right food choices…

I choose natural whole food…

I choose natural whole food…

I choose natural whole food…

Fruits and vegetables make up most of my food intake…

Fruits and vegetables make up most of my food intake…

Fruits and vegetables make up most of my food intake…

I never crash diet as I know they don't work…

I never crash diet as I know they don't work…

I never crash diet as I know they don't work…

I don't need to count calories as my mind keeps me thin….

I don't need to count calories as my mind keeps me thin….

I don't need to count calories as my mind keeps me thin....

I don't need to count calories as my mind knows how to burn off unwanted fat....

I don't need to count calories as my mind knows how to burn off unwanted fat....

I don't need to count calories as my mind knows how to burn off unwanted fat....

My mind knows how to burn off unwanted fat...

My mind knows how to burn off unwanted fat...

My mind knows how to burn off unwanted fat...

My body is a fat burning machine...

My body is a fat burning machine...

My body is a fat burning machine...

My body is a fat burning machine...

I live my life with love in my heart...

I live my life with love in my heart...

I live my life with love in my heart...

Rapid Weight Loss Hypnosis

I focus on positive emotions and energy...
I focus on positive emotions and energy...
I focus on positive emotions and energy...

I surround myself with other positive people...
I surround myself with other positive people...
I surround myself with other positive people...

Everyone in my world helps me to be thin...
Everyone in my world helps me to be thin...
Everyone in my world helps me to be thin...

My life is focused on being super healthy...
My life is focused on being super healthy...
My life is focused on being super healthy...

I am naturally thin as a result of my lifestyle...
I am naturally thin as a result of my lifestyle...
I am naturally thin as a result of my lifestyle...

My food choices keeps me thin...

My food choices keeps me thin...

My food choices keeps me thin...

When I think of myself, I see a thin and healthy person...

When I think of myself, I see a thin and healthy person...

When I think of myself, I see a thin and healthy person...

My body is just how I want to be...

My body is just how I want to be...

My body is just how I want to be...

I want to shape my body through exercise and a more active lifestyle...

I want to shape my body through exercise and a more active lifestyle...

I want to shape my body through exercise and a more active lifestyle...

I visualize myself as a fit and healthy me that I am...

I visualize myself as a fit and healthy me that I am...

I visualize myself as a fit and healthy me that I am...

Every day, I meditate to focus on being fit and healthy...

Every day, I meditate to focus on being fit and healthy...

Every day, I meditate to focus on being fit and healthy...

I want to be thin and healthy...

I want to be thin and healthy...

I want to be thin and healthy...

Whatever that held me back in the past is no longer an issue...

Whatever that held me back in the past is no longer an issue...

Whatever that held me back in the past is no longer an issue…

I have decided to live like a naturally thin person…

I have decided to live like a naturally thin person…

I have decided to live like a naturally thin person…

Because I think of myself as thin, my mind and body responds…

Because I think of myself as thin, my mind and body responds…

Because I think of myself as thin, my mind and body responds…

My mind keeps my body thin…

My mind keeps my body thin…

My mind keeps my body thin…

I love eating food that keep me safe…

I love eating food that keep me safe...

I love eating food that keep me safe...

I love eating food that keep me thin...

I love eating food that keep me thin...

I love eating food that keep me thin...

I enjoy eating nutritious food...

I enjoy eating nutritious food...

I enjoy eating nutritious food...

Natural, whole food are my favorite...

Natural, whole food are my favorite...

Natural, whole food are my favorite...

I will encourage my family and friends to eat whole foods as well...

I will encourage my family and friends to eat whole foods as well...

I will encourage my family and friends to eat whole foods as well...

I easily say no to food that are processed...
I easily say no to food that are processed...
I easily say no to food that are processed...

Processed foods do not enter into my mouth...
Processed foods do not enter into my mouth...
Processed foods do not enter into my mouth...

I feel sick when eating processed food...
I feel sick when eating processed food...
I feel sick when eating processed food...

I can easily reject food that don't keep me thin...
I can easily reject food that don't keep me thin...
I can easily reject food that don't keep me thin...

If it isn't food from nature, I don't eat it...
If it isn't food from nature, I don't eat it...
If it isn't food from nature, I don't eat it...

If it's food out of the factory, I say no to it...

If it's food out of the factory, I say no to it...

If it's food out of the factory, I say no to it...

I love the fact that there are so many natural health food options...

I love the fact that there are so many natural health food options...

I love the fact that there are so many natural health food options...

I can't wait to eat more nutritious food...

I can't wait to eat more nutritious food...

I can't wait to eat more nutritious food...

I can't wait to see more nutritious food...

I can't wait to see more nutritious food...

I can't wait to see more nutritious food...

I eat as much natural whole food as I want until I'm full...

I eat as much natural whole food as I want until I'm full...

I eat as much natural whole food as I want until I'm full…

I stop eating when I am full…

I stop eating when I am full…

I stop eating when I am full…

I am thin and healthy today…

I am thin and healthy today…

I am thin and healthy today…

I am so happy about being a naturally thin person…

I am so happy about being a naturally thin person…

I am so happy about being a naturally thin person…

I love my life as a naturally thin person…

I love my life as a naturally thin person…

I love my life as a naturally thin person…

It's natural for me being thin...

It's natural for me being thin...

It's natural for me being thin...

I focus my thoughts on living like a naturally thin person...

I focus my thoughts on living like a naturally thin person...

I focus my thoughts on living like a naturally thin person...

Thin and healthy are natural for me...

Thin and healthy are natural for me...

Thin and healthy are natural for me...

I only think of loving and positive thoughts about myself...

I only think of loving and positive thoughts about myself...

I only think of loving and positive thoughts about myself...

I am focused on keeping myself healthy...

I am focused on keeping myself healthy...

I am focused on keeping myself healthy...

When I eat out, I always find food that support my health...

When I eat out, I always find food that support my health...

When I eat out, I always find food that support my health...

I instinctively know which are the healthy food options...

I instinctively know which are the healthy food options...

I instinctively know which are the healthy food options...

I drink fresh and clean water...

I drink fresh and clean water...

I drink fresh and clean water...

I eliminate all sugar from my food...
I eliminate all sugar from my food...
I eliminate all sugar from my food...

I eliminate all processed food...
I eliminate all processed food...
I eliminate all processed food...

I eliminate all fatty food...
I eliminate all fatty food...
I eliminate all fatty food...

I am highly selective about what I eat...
I am highly selective about what I eat...
I am highly selective about what I eat...

I make wise food choices...
I make wise food choices...
I make wise food choices...

I have a clear picture in my mind of the healthiest in me...

I have a clear picture in my mind of the healthiest in me...

I have a clear picture in my mind of the healthiest in me...

I think thin today...

I think thin today...

I think thin today...

I am healthy today...

I am healthy today...

I am healthy today...

I am naturally thin...

I am naturally thin...

I am naturally thin...

I feel comfortable being thin...

I feel comfortable being thin...

I feel comfortable being thin...

I feel comfortable being healthy...

I feel comfortable being healthy...

I feel comfortable being healthy...

I appreciate the extra energy that comes from eating healthy...

I appreciate the extra energy that comes from eating healthy...

I appreciate the extra energy that comes from eating healthy...

I am ecstatic by how good looking I am now...

I am ecstatic by how good looking I am now...

I am ecstatic by how good looking I am now...

When I look in the mirror, I notice the positive improvements in myself...

When I look in the mirror, I notice the positive improvements in myself...

When I look in the mirror, I notice the positive improvements in myself...

I enjoy hearing all positive comments from those who notice my healthy body...

I enjoy hearing all positive comments from those who notice my healthy body...

I enjoy hearing all positive comments from those who notice my healthy body...

I only speak about the new thin and healthy me...

I only speak about the new thin and healthy me...

I only speak about the new thin and healthy me...

I don't look back in the past because I am excited about the future...

I don't look back in the past because I am excited about the future...

I don't look back in the past because I am excited about the future...

I see a thin and healthy person in the future...

I see a thin and healthy person in the future...

I see a thin and healthy person in the future...

I love the new healthy me...

I love the new healthy me...

I love the new healthy me...

I love myself today...

I love myself today...

I love myself today...

My body automatically shifts to being naturally slim...

My body automatically shifts to being naturally slim...

My body automatically shifts to being naturally slim...

My body knows what my natural state is...

My body knows what my natural state is...

My body knows what my natural state is...

My mind is focused on maintaining my ideal weight…

My mind is focused on maintaining my ideal weight…

My mind is focused on maintaining my ideal weight…

My mind churns up my metabolism to melt away any unwanted fat…

My mind churns up my metabolism to melt away any unwanted fat…

My mind churns up my metabolism to melt away any unwanted fat…

I am emotionally strong…

I am emotionally strong…

I am emotionally strong…

I am confident in myself…

I am confident in myself…

I am confident in myself…

I know I can achieve the goals I set my mind to...

I know I can achieve the goals I set my mind to...

I know I can achieve the goals I set my mind to...

I can live life on my terms...

I can live life on my terms...

I can live life on my terms...

I can be thin and healthy...

I can be thin and healthy...

I can be thin and healthy...

I focus on being healthy all the time...

I focus on being healthy all the time...

I focus on being healthy all the time...

My mind is now geared to think only of healthy and positive thoughts...

My mind is now geared to think only of healthy and positive thoughts...

My mind is now geared to think only of healthy and positive thoughts...

I make choices that support me being feeling healthy...

I make choices that support me being feeling healthy...

I make choices that support me being feeling healthy...

I am naturally thin and healthy...

I am naturally thin and healthy...

I am naturally thin and healthy...

Positive Affirmations to Keep Exercise Motivation

Regular exercise is an important component of weight loss.

If you need an extra push to exercise or if you want to listen to positive affirmations in the gym, you can listen to the following autosuggestions that are designed to help you maximize the results of your workout sessions.

They're quite easy to follow along. They will remind you of how amazing you really are.

As you work hard towards your weight loss goal, you can contemplate on the following:

I am amazing...

I am amazing...

I am amazing...

My body is a work of art...

My body is a work of art...

My body is a work of art...

I am a miracle...

I am a miracle...

I am a miracle...

I am determined to fulfill my destiny...

I am determined to fulfill my destiny...

I am determined to fulfill my destiny...

I am capable of achieving my health goals...

I am capable of achieving my health goals...
I am capable of achieving my health goals...

I can do this...
I can do this...
I can do this...

I am capable of achieving great things...
I am capable of achieving great things...
I am capable of achieving great things...

I can do this...
I can do this...
I can do this...

I feel amazing whenever I exercise...
I feel amazing whenever I exercise...
I feel amazing whenever I exercise...

My body is wonderful...
My body is wonderful...

My body is wonderful...

My body is powerful...
My body is powerful...
My body is powerful...

My body is strong...
My body is strong....
My body is strong...

I can do this...
I can do this...
I can do this...

My mind is powerful...
My mind is powerful...
My mind is powerful...

I have a strong body and mind...
I have a strong body and mind...
I have a strong body and mind...

I have come this far so I will not quit...
I have come this far so I will not quit...
I have come this far so I will not quit...

I am capable of doing things...
I am capable of doing things...
I am capable of doing things...

I focus on the positive...
I focus on the positive...
I focus on the positive...

I focus on what my body can do...
I focus on what my body can do...
I focus on what my body can do...

I need exercise so I can be healthier...
I need exercise so I can be healthier...
I need exercise so I can be healthier...

I am doing this so I can be strong...

I am doing this so I can be strong...

I am doing this so I can be strong...

I have come this far so I will not quit...

I have come this far so I will not quit...

I have come this far so I will not quit...

I am doing this to improve the quality of my life...

I am doing this to improve the quality of my life...

I am doing this to improve the quality of my life...

My body is becoming fit and healthy...

My body is becoming fit and healthy...

My body is becoming fit and healthy...

I am doing this to get stronger and more powerful...

I am doing this to get stronger and more powerful...

I am doing this to get stronger and more powerful...

I am doing this for myself…

I am doing this for myself…

I am doing this for myself…

I focus on my workout…

I focus on my workout…

I focus on my workout…

As you focus on your workout, visualize who you truly are. You are being filled with light and radiance. There's more to you than meets the eye.

Feel the energy radiating from your body…

Feel the warmth spreading into the universe…

See your light radiating into the universe…

You are highly capable of achieving great things…

You are doing this to get stronger and more powerful…

You are doing this for yourself…

Focus on your workout...

Feel the light and radiance...

Feel the warmth of this radiance as it emanates from you...

Feel the warmth spreading into the universe...

See your light radiating into the universe...

You can do this...

You are a beam of light and energy...

You are doing it so your body will be healthy...

You are doing this for your body to be strong...

You can do this...

You are capable of achieving great things...

No matter how tough it is...

No matter how much it takes...

You can do this...

Follow along...

I am healthy and strong...

I am healthy and strong...

I am healthy and strong...

My body is powerful...
My body is powerful...
My body is powerful...

I can do anything you want to do...
I can do anything you want to do...
I can do anything you want to do...

I can do this...
I can do this...
I can do this...

I can eat properly and I can sustain regular exercise...
I can eat properly and I can sustain regular exercise...
I can eat properly and I can sustain regular exercise...

My body is a miracle...
My body is a miracle...

My body is a miracle...

I am determined to fulfill my destiny...
I am determined to fulfill my destiny...
I am determined to fulfill my destiny...

I am a miracle...
I am a miracle...
I am a miracle...

My body is healthy and strong...
My body is healthy and strong...
My body is healthy and strong...

Every moment I'm getting stronger...
Every moment I'm getting stronger...
Every moment I'm getting stronger...

Every moment I'm getting better...
Every moment I'm getting better...
Every moment I'm getting better...

I am getting faster every day...

I am getting faster every day...

I am getting faster every day...

My body is healthy and strong...

My body is healthy and strong...

My body is healthy and strong...

People will notice how strong and healthy I look...

People will notice how strong and healthy I look...

People will notice how strong and healthy I look...

People will notice how powerful my body is...

People will notice how powerful my body is...

People will notice how powerful my body is...

I feel stronger every day...

I feel stronger every day...

Rapid Weight Loss Hypnosis

I feel stronger every day...

My body is a mirror...
My body is a mirror...
My body is a mirror...

My mind is powerful and strong...
My mind is powerful and strong...
My mind is powerful and strong...

My body is amazing...
My body is amazing...
My body is amazing...

I am healthy and strong...
I am healthy and strong...
I am healthy and strong...

I am determined to fulfill my destiny...
I am determined to fulfill my destiny...
I am determined to fulfill my destiny...

I will not waste my only chance in life...

I will not waste my only chance in life...

I will not waste my only chance in life...

I will do this the right way...

I will do this the right way...

I will do this the right way...

I am amazing...

I am amazing...

I am amazing...

My body is amazing...

My body is amazing...

My body is amazing...

I believe in no pain, no gain...

I believe in no pain, no gain...

I believe in no pain, no gain...

Suffer now and forever be a champion...

Suffer now and forever be a champion...

Suffer now and forever be a champion...

My mind is now wiring up to prepare my body towards weight loss...

My mind is now wiring up to prepare my body towards weight loss...

My mind is now wiring up to prepare my body towards weight loss...

I can do this...

I can do this...

I can do this...

Chapter 6 - Additional Tips for Weight Loss

While hypnosis and positive affirmations can improve your chances to lose weight and become the person you visualize you want to be, there are more things you can add to your plan to help you finally achieve your goals.

Here are additional tips to help you lose weight fast.

Eat More Fruits and Vegetables

Fruits and vegetables have several beneficial properties that can help you lose weight. They contain a lot of fiber and minimal calories.

They are also rich in water that provides them with low energy density, which makes them quite filling compared to other food groups.

Eat More Protein

Protein is an important nutrient that can help you lose weight. Adding more protein to your daily meals can help you boost metabolism between 70 and 110 calories every day.

One study also discovered that consuming more protein may result in a reduction in appetite especially late at night.

Try Intermittent Fasting

Like hypnotherapy, intermittent fasting is also now gaining ground among people who want to try an alternative treatment for losing weight. In this eating cycle, you have to follow a period of fasting, and then periods of feasting.

Studies suggest that this eating pattern is also effective for weight management as it is easier to manage calorie intake by skipping some meals.

Moreover, it may also reduce muscle mass loss, which is usually linked with diets that are based on low calories.

Cut Down on Sugary Drinks

You are now probably aware of the bad effects of sugar on our health. You should avoid sweetened food, especially sweet drinks. One study shows that the calories from drinks that are high in sugar might be the highest contributor to the current problem of obesity. So stay away from soda, artificial fruit juices, and unhealthy smoothies.

Lift Weights

Aside from cardio exercises, you should also add weightlifting to your exercise regimen. One of the side effects of dieting is a slowdown in metabolism and muscle loss. To prevent this, you should perform some type of resistance exercises such as weight lifting. Studies reveal that lifting weights can help you maintain your high metabolism and prevent you from losing muscle mass.

Get Enough Sleep

Getting enough sleep at night (at least 7 to 8 hours of continuous sleep) is also crucial as a healthy diet and exercise. Studies reveal that lack of sleep is one of the highest risk factors for obesity both in adults and in children.

Conclusion

Thanks again for taking the time to listen to this book!

By now, you should have a good understanding of hypnosis and positive affirmations, and how these effective strategies can help you improve your chances to finally become a healthier version of yourself.

Through the power of hypnotism and positive words, you can rewire your mind so your body can understand that certain activities and restrictions are important to help you lose weight.

You will start viewing exercise not as a physical burden but as a work process that will help you become healthier.

And of course, through hypnosis, you can reframe your mindset to accept the reality that some food groups, despite being delicious, are just not healthy for us.

In fact, diet is more important in certain aspects of weight loss. For example, if you want to get abs, you need to focus on your diet and not with your training.

Even if you train in the gym for long hours every day, you cannot get your abs appearing if you don't discipline yourself.

Hypnotism for weight loss is only effective if you exert an equal amount of energy towards execution - watching your diet and regular exercise.

If you enjoyed this book, please take the time to leave me a review on the platform. I appreciate your honest feedback, and it really helps me to continue producing high-quality books.

Thank you

Before you go, I just wanted to say thank you for purchasing my book.

You could have picked from dozens of other books on the same topic but you took a chance and chose this one.

So, a HUGE thanks to you for getting this book and for reading all the way to the end.

Now I wanted to ask you for a small favor. ***Could you please consider posting a review on the platform? Reviews are one of the easiest ways to support the work of independent authors.***

This feedback will help me continue to write the type of books that will help you get the results you want. So if you enjoyed it, please let me know.

Lastly, don't forget to grab a copy of your Free Bonus - my complete *Law of Attraction: Attract What You Desire* Boxset. If you want to learn how to harness the amazing magic of the Law of Attraction to manifest anything you want, this boxset is for you.

Just go to:

https://theartofmastery.com/loa

www.ingramcontent.com/pod-product-compliance
Lightning Source LLC
Chambersburg PA
CBHW052101110526
44591CB00013B/2307